How to Reach Your Favorite Superstar

▼▼▼▼

*By Larry P. Stevens
and Cara J. Stevens*

LOWELL HOUSE JUVENILE

LOS ANGELES

NTC/Contemporary Publishing Group

Published by Lowell House
A division of NTC/Contemporary Publishing Group, Inc.
4255 West Touhy Avenue, Lincolnwood (Chicago),
Illinois 60646-1975 U.S.A.

Managing Director and Publisher: Jack Artenstein
Director of Publishing Services: Rena Copperman
Editorial Director: Brenda Pope-Ostrow
Director of Juvenile Development: Amy Downing
Typesetter: Justin Segal

Lowell House books can be purchased at special discounts
when ordered in bulk for premiums and special sales.
Please contact Customer Service at:
NTC/Contemporary Publishing Group
4255 W. Touhy Avenue
Lincolnwood, IL 60646-1975
1-800-323-4900

Printed and bound in the United States of America

ISBN: 0-7373-0332-8

OPM
1 2 3 4 5 6 7 8 9 10

Contents

Reach out and get in touch with someone!

Your favorite stars work hard to give you hours of entertainment—and they love to hear that you appreciate their efforts. If you've ever had the impulse to tell a special celeb exactly how you feel, now is the time to do it!

But how do you reach your favorite star? This book will show you how. So read about your favorite celebrities in the following pages, then get out your stationery and write on! And remember these pointers for best results:

➤ If you want a reply, it's best to send a self-addressed, stamped envelope (SASE) along with your letter. That's an envelope that is stamped with the proper postage and has your own name and address printed legibly on it.

➤ If you are writing to or from a country other than the United States (for instance, if you are in Canada and writing to a star at a U.S. address), you will need international postage coupons, because a simple SASE won't work in other countries. By including the postage coupons, which are available at any post office, you'll have a better chance of receiving a reply.

➤ Not all celebrities have fan clubs. When you send your letter, you might want to request fan club information—or, if you feel like you've got the time and devotion, you could inquire about setting up a fan club for that star yourself!

➤ Always remember that celebrities change addresses, just like anybody else. They move, go on location for months, or change agents. But even if the person you write to decides to move, your letter should be forwarded to the new address.

Ben Affleck

*A*s a young kid in Boston, Ben was asked by a family friend to play a small part in an independent film. Ben accepted the offer and never looked back. He dove headfirst into acting to become one of the hottest young stars on the planet. Ben and his childhood pal Matt Damon have taken Hollywood by storm. Of course, like any actor, Ben has had his ups and downs. His earliest career disappointment was getting the lead in a film called *Atuk* when he was 16, only to have it shut down in the middle of production. Taking it in his usual stride, Ben didn't miss a beat and got right on with his acting. Today, Ben's a shining star as writer, director, and actor, charming everyone who sees him on the big screen or in person.

Birthday Beat
August 15, 1972

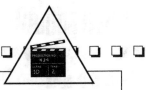

So You Want to Know—

What Ben would change about himself? "I'd make myself a simpler person. I think about too many things at once. I'd make myself more singular of purpose, instead of having so many disparate interests. And I'd make myself less a compulsive consumer. I tend to like to spend money. I get into photography, so I buy a bunch of cameras. I like to ride a motorcycle, so I bought three motorcycles."

Cool Credits

➤ TV debut: *The Voyage of the Mimi*, PBS
➤ Film: *Dazed and Confused, Mallrats, Chasing Amy, Going All the Way, Phantoms, Good Will Hunting, Armageddon, Shakespeare in Love, Forces of Nature*
➤ Won the 1997 Golden Globe and Academy Award for Best Screenplay, *Good Will Hunting*

Super Stats

➤ Birthplace: Berkeley, California
➤ Raised in: Massachusetts
➤ Current residence: Hollywood, California
➤ Car: a black '69 Cadillac
➤ Family: younger brother, Casey, also an actor, born during Ben's third birthday party; parents are an educator and a drug/alcohol counselor

• •

Ben Affleck
10100 Santa Monica Blvd., Ste. 2500
Los Angeles, CA 90067

7

• •

Tatyana Ali

Cool Credits

➤ TV: *Sesame Street*, 1983–87; co-host of two Saturday morning programs: *Name Your Adventure* and *Brains and Brawn*; played Ashley Banks on *The Fresh Prince of Bel Air*, appeared on *The Cosby Show, Hawk, All My Children*, and the British TV series *Family Album*; two-time winner on *Star Search*

➤ Film: *Mr. Foster's Field Trip, Kidz in the Wood*

➤ Album: *Kiss the Sky*

Super Stats

➤ Full name: Tatyana Marisol Ali

➤ Birthplace: Long Island, New York

➤ Current residence: Los Angeles

➤ Family: father, Sheriff, is a retired New York City police detective; mother, Sonia, is a nurse; two younger sisters, Anastasia and Kimberly

➤ Heritage: father is a native of Trinidad; mother is from Panama

➤ Hobbies: gymnastics, singing, dancing, and swimming

➤ Education: graduated high school with honors; deferred admission to Harvard University so she can work on her singing career

Birthday Beat
January 24, 1979

*S*he's only 20 years old, but Tatyana has been acting for 16 years. Her life-long dedication to her craft shines through in all her performances, whether they're on television, on stage, or on the big screen. The secret to her success is honesty and confidence. Tatyana feels every word that she sings and speaks, and the audience can't help but feel them right along with her.

So You Want to Know—

How Tatyana made the leap from actor to singing star? It was friend and co-star Will Smith who convinced Tatyana to pursue her singing professionally. His belief in Tatyana's talent was so strong, he signed her to his production company, Will Smith Enterprises. When asked why, Smith jokes, "Because she's almost as talented as I am." With his help, Tatyana prepared a demo and eventually signed with MJJ Music. Tatyana's response to Will's help is heartfelt. "He really believes in me. It's nice to have people around you who think highly of you."

Tatyana Ali
4924 Balboa Blvd., #377
Encino, CA 91316-3402

Backstreet Boys

■ ■ ■ ■ ■ ■ ■ ■ ■ ■ ■ ■ ■ ■ ■

While living in Orlando, Florida, back in 1995, AJ McLean, Howie Dorough, and Nick Carter kept running into each other at local acting auditions. They struck up a fast friendship and decided to form a band. They invited their friend Kevin Richardson to join. Kevin brought along his cousin Brian Littrell, and the Boys were ready to rock! They signed with manager Donna Wright, who believed in them so strongly that she immediately called David McPherson of Jive Records. She held up her cell phone while the Boys were rehearsing. David recognized a great thing when he heard it and got the group signed right away.

Birthday Beat

AJ: January 9, 1978
Brian: February 20, 1975
Howie: August 22, 1973
Kevin: October 3, 1972
Nick: January 28, 1980

So You Want to Know—

What the Boys like to eat when they're on the road? Whenever they're in a foreign city, Howie and Kevin like to try the local food, while Nick, Brian, and AJ search for the closest McDonald's.

Cool Credits

➤ Won the 1996 and 1997 MTV Europe "Viewer's Choice" Award
➤ Won the 1998 MTV Music Video Award for Best Group Video
➤ Won the 1998 *Billboard* Music Awards for Best Group and Best Adult-Contemporary Group
➤ Won four 1999 World Music Awards for World's Best-Selling Pop Group, R&B Group, Dance Group, and American Group

Super Stats

➤ Birthplaces: AJ—West Palm Beach, Florida; Howie—Orlando, Florida; Kevin—Lexington, Kentucky; Nick— Jamestown, New York; Brian—Lexington, Kentucky
➤ Nicknames: Brian— B-Rok; AJ—Bone; Howie—Sweet-D
➤ Fave foods: Brian— macaroni and cheese; AJ—McDonald's; Howie—Asian; Kevin—Mexican and Asian; Nick—McDonald's and pizza

Backstreet Boys
c/o Jive Records
137-139 W. 25th St.
New York, NY 10001
Official Web site: www.backstreetboys.com

Tyra Banks

When 18-year-old Tyra Banks walked into an L.A. modeling agency at the urging of her classmates, she had no idea that one nonpaying job would lead to a flourishing career in acting and modeling. After a year in Paris modeling high fashion, she returned to the States and continued to work, landing a recurring role on the hit TV comedy *The Fresh Prince of Bel Air*. With film, TV, and tons of modeling credits under her belt, what is Tyra's dream role? "I would love to play a singer [in a movie]. But...I'll leave the singing to Whitney Houston, Mariah Carey, [and] Celine Dion."

So You Want to Know—

What Tyra does when she's not in front of the camera? Tyra's favorite charity is Children + Families, an organization dedicated to helping abused and neglected kids. The series Cards from the Heart by Tyra's Kidsuccess Kids was created by 8- and 9-year-olds in an after-school program. The project is designed to enhance literacy for children living in troubled environments.

Super Stats

➤ Height: 5'11"
➤ Hair: brown
➤ Eyes: hazel
➤ Birthplace: Los Angeles, California
➤ Agency: IMG Models
➤ Honors: one of *People* magazine's Most Beautiful People in the World, 1996
➤ Fave causes: the rain forests and education

Cool Credits

➤ Film: *Higher Learning, A Woman Like That, Love Stinks*
➤ TV: *The Fresh Prince of Bel Air* (as Jackie), *New York Undercover, Inferno*
➤ Book: *Tyra's Beauty*
➤ First African-American Maybelline cover girl at age 20

➤ First African-American woman to make the cover of *Sports Illustrated*'s swimsuit issue

Tyra Banks
c/o IMG
170 5th Ave., 10th Floor
New York, NY 10010

Drew Barrymore

▼▼▼▼▼▼▼▼▼▼▼▼▼▼▼▼▼▼▼

Drew's early start in show business came at age 2, when she appeared in TV commercials. A child star from a family of actors who flew from one box office smash to another, Drew's star-studded life became too much for her, and she fell into a life of drugs and addiction before she was a teen. After a tough rehabilitation at age 14 and writing a cleansing auto-biography in 1989, she was ready to start a new life. With more acting and even producing credits to her name, Drew's definitely back on top.

Birthday Beat
February 22, 1975

So You Want to Know—

If Drew will continue to play more fun and fantasy roles, or will she turn to the dramatic anytime soon? She wants her characters to represent where she is in her life. "I don't want to do anything heavy. I just want to laugh."

Cool Credits

➤ Autobiography: *Little Girl Lost*
➤ Film highlights: *Bogie, Altered States, E.T. The Extra-Terrestrial, Firestarter, Irreconcilable Differences, Cat's Eye, See You in the Morning, Far from Home, Poison Ivy, Wayne's World 2, Bad Girls, Mad Love, Batman Forever, Boys on the Side, Everyone Says I Love You, Scream, Home Fries, Best Men, Ever After, The Wedding Singer, Never Been Kissed* (also executive producer)

Super Stats

➤ Birthplace: Los Angeles, California
➤ Family: grandfather is actor John Barrymore; dad is John Drew Barrymore
➤ Extended family: godfather is Steven Spielberg; goddaughter is Frances Bean Cobain, Courtney Love's daughter
➤ Fave charity: the Wildlife Waystation in Los Angeles
➤ Dislikes: chocolate

• •

Drew Barrymore
c/o Studio Fan Mail
1122 S. Robertson Blvd., #15
Los Angeles, CA 90035

• •

Brandy

Super Stats

➤ Full name: Brandy Norwood
➤ Birthplace: McComb, Mississippi
➤ Education: currently attending Pepperdine University, Los Angeles
➤ Current residence: San Fernando Valley suburbs with her mom, dad, and brother, Ray J.
➤ Family: mom, Sonja, is her manager; dad, Willie Sr., is her vocal teacher and inspiration
➤ Fave star: Whitney Houston
➤ Fave singers: Celine Dion and Jewel
➤ Fave movies: *Titanic, The Game, Devil's Advocate*
➤ Suffers from: stage fright

Cool Credits

➤ Film: *Arachnophobia, I Still Know What You Did Last Summer*
➤ TV: the TV movies *Rodgers & Hammerstein's Cinderella,* and *Double Platinum* with Diana Ross; the series *Thea* and *Moesha*
➤ Albums: *Brandy, Never Say Never*

So You Want to Know—

If Brandy wants people to see her as the girl next door? "I'm nice [but] I make mistakes and I hurt like everyone else. I'm just trying to tell everybody, 'Hey, I'm not Miss Perfect. I rebel like every other teenager.'" Brandy feels that she can play more than the teenager next door. She feels she suffers from a "good-girl image."

■ ■ ■ ■ ■ ■ ■ ■ ■ ■ ■ ■ ■ ■ ■ ■ ■

*G*rowing up singing gospel music with her father, Brandy knew at age 4½ that she wanted to be a singer. With her parents' support, Brandy skyrocketed to success, hitting the *Billboard* Top 10 at age 15. This young renaissance woman can do it all: She stars in her own TV show, *Moesha,* and has appeared in several films and TV movies in addition to keeping up with  her rising music career. She has achieved gold and platinum status on four of her hits.

Birthday Beat
February 11, 1979

• •

Brandy
c/o Atlantic Records
9229 Sunset Blvd., #900
Los Angeles, CA 90069

17
• •

Kobe Bryant

Born and raised in Philadelphia, Pennsylvania, Kobe lived in Italy for eight years and learned to speak fluent Italian. Kobe currently resides in Los Angeles, where he plays for the Los Angeles Lakers. He dreamed of following in his father's footsteps and becoming a professional basketball player. He went straight from high school to the pros, skipping college after being named Player of the Year in 1996. Kobe continues to be one of the most exciting and popular young stars in the NBA.

So You Want to Know—

Who was the most influential person in Kobe's basketball career? "My father always played with a great love for the game, and that's one of the things he always taught me, especially after I made the jump to the NBA," says Kobe. "He told me not to let the pressure or the expectations take away from my love for the game, and I think that's the best advice anyone's ever given me."

Birthday Beat
August 23, 1978

Super Stats

➤ Height: 6'7"
➤ Weight: 215
➤ Birthplace: Philadelphia
➤ Started playing basketball: age 5
➤ Where his name came from: His parents named him after a type of steak on a restaurant menu
➤ Family: father, Joe "Jelly Bean" Bryant, averaged 8.7 ppg in 606 career games in the NBA; two older sisters, Sharia and Shaya
➤ Fave movie: *Star Wars*

Cool Credits

➤ Selected by the Charlotte Hornets in first round (13th pick overall) of 1996 NBA draft
➤ NBA All-Rookie Second Team, 1997
➤ Selected by *USA Today* and *Parade* magazine as the National High School Player of the Year, 1996
➤ Youngest player to start an NBA game, 1997
➤ Won the NBA Slam Dunk Contest, 1997
➤ Starter for the 1998 All-Star Game, becoming at 19 the youngest all-star in NBA history

Kobe Bryant
c/o Los Angeles Lakers
3900 W. Manchester Blvd.
P.O. Box 10
Inglewood, CA 90305-2227

Terrell Davis

▼▼▼▼▼▼▼▼▼▼▼▼▼▼▼▼▼▼▼▼▼▼▼

I n just five seasons in the NFL, Terrell has already set 47 team records, captured two Super Bowl rings, and received a Super Bowl MVP award. Each game is a triumph for Terrell, who suffers from debilitating migraine headaches. He continues to lead the Broncos to victory and earn himself and the team a place in the record books.

So You Want to Know—

What Terrell's hidden talent is? As part of *Sesame Street*'s 30th season celebration, Terrell joined his Muppet friends for a special guest appearance. The NFL's leading rusher recited the alphabet while being cheered on by Telly Monster, Baby Bear, and Elmo. Terrell, who admits that his favorite letters are T and D, confided to Oscar the Grouch that his next three favorite letters are M, V, and P.

Super Stats

➤ Team: Denver Broncos (running back)
➤ Height: 5'11"
➤ Weight: 210
➤ Birthplace: San Diego, California
➤ Current residence: Aurora, Colorado
➤ Family: mother, Kateree; brothers, Joe, James, Bobby, and Terry
➤ Nickname: Boss Hogg
➤ Fave sport (other than football): bowling
➤ College: University of Georgia
➤ Hobbies: playing Sega video games, especially Madden Football '99; also likes to watch basketball
➤ Fave foods: soul food, cheesecake
➤ Fave animal: alligator
➤ Charity: started the Terrell Davis Foundation for Migraine Education and Treatment

Cool Credits

➤ 19 100 Yard + rushing games
➤ Holds Super Bowl single-game record for most rushing touchdowns: 3 (January 25, 1998, vs. Green Bay)
➤ Shares Super Bowl single-game record for most points: 18 (January 25, 1998, vs. Green Bay)
➤ Holds NFL postseason career record for highest average gain: 5.33
➤ Super Bowl MVP, 1998

Birthday Beat
October 28, 1972

Terrell Davis
c/o Denver Broncos
13655 Broncos Pkwy.
Englewood, CO 80112

Tim Duncan

*T*im was identified as a rising basketball star when a Wake Forest University alumnus was visiting his home of St. Croix on a goodwill mission to promote the NBA in the Caribbean. Although Georgetown, Providence, and Delaware all tried to recruit Tim, he ultimately decided to attend Wake Forest in 1993. Although he could have left Wake Forest after his junior year to become the No. 1 pick in the NBA draft, he decided to complete his degree in psychology to fulfill a promise he had made. Before her death, Tim's mother had each of her children promise to earn a college degree, which they all did. Upon graduation, Tim was drafted to play for the San Antonio Spurs.

Birthday Beat
April 25, 1976

So You Want to Know—

Did Tim always want to be a basketball star? Actually, Tim wanted to follow in the footsteps of his older sister, Tricia, who swam for the United States in the 1988 Olympic Games. By the time Tim was 14, he had become a top U.S. competitor in the 400-meter freestyle. In 1989, Hurricane Hugo hit his home, St. Croix, with such power and force that it destroyed all of the swimming pools on the island. He turned to basketball and is now one of the best players in the world.

Super Stats

➤ Full name: Timothy Theodore Duncan
➤ Height: 7'
➤ Weight: 248
➤ Shoe size: 16
➤ Birthplace: St. Croix, U.S. Virgin Islands
➤ Education: graduated in 1997 with a B.A. in psychology from Wake Forest University in North Carolina

Cool Credits

➤ NCAA all-American, 1995–97; No. 1 pick in 1997 NBA draft
➤ NCAA Player of the Year, 1997
➤ NBA Rookie of the Year, 1998
➤ Only rookie to play in 1998 NBA All-Star Game
➤ MVP of NBA Championship series, 1999

Tim Duncan
c/o San Antonio Spurs
100 Montana St.
San Antonio, TX 78203-1031

Calista Flockhart

Cool Credits

➤ TV: the TV movies *An American Story* and Darrow; title role on the series *Ally McBeal*
➤ Film: *Quiz Show, Naked in New York, The Birdcage, Drunks, Telling Lies in America, A Midsummer Night's Dream*

Super Stats

➤ Birthplace: Freeport, Illinois
➤ Raised in: Medford, New Jersey
➤ Current residence: Los Angeles, California

➤ Family: mother was a schoolteacher; father was a quality-control executive with Kraft Foods
➤ Friends: actor Ben Stiller and director Sam Hendes
➤ Fun fact: *Calista* means "beautiful" in Greek
➤ Loves: hiking; adores the nature aspect of Los Angeles after moving there from New York
➤ Fave sport: kickboxing
➤ Fave store: The Gap
➤ Fave clothes: her white drawstring pajamas

24

Birthday Beat
November 11, 1964

*U*nder the scrutiny of the public eye since her hit TV show *Ally McBeal* went on the air, Calista has not bowed to pressure from the media or from anyone else for that matter. In fact, Calista feels it has made her even stronger. When people stare at her on the street, she stares right back, unruffled. "I've stared at people my whole life. When I was a kid, my mother would tell me to stop it." When the press got their knickers in a twist over the length of her miniskirts, Calista said, "It just made me wear them shorter."

Calista Flockhart
c/o The Gersh Agency
P.O. Box 5617
Beverly Hills, CA 90210

Brendan Fraser

Cool Credits

➤ Film highlights: *Dogfight, Encino Man, School Ties, Twenty Bucks, Airheads, With Honors, Now and Then, Mrs. Winterbourne, Still Breathing, The Twilight of the Golds, George of the Jungle, Gods and Monsters, The Mummy, Blast from the Past, Dudley Do-Right*
➤ TV: the TV movies *Child of Darkness, Child of Light* and *Guilty Until Proven Innocent*
➤ Won the Golden Space Needle Award for Best Actor at the 1997 Seattle International Film Festival for *Still Breathing*

Birthday Beat

December 3, 1968

Super Stats

➤ Birthplace: Indianapolis, Indiana
➤ Raised in: Canada, Holland, London, and Switzerland
➤ Education: graduated from Cornish College of the Arts in Seattle
➤ Family: three older brothers; wife, actress Afton Smith
➤ Hobbies: fencing, mime, juggling, and photography
➤ Enjoys: all sorts of dance, especially ballet, modern, jazz, and ballroom

Although capable of doing both drama and slapstick comedy, Brendan seems to seek roles that display his two best qualities: silliness and sexiness. Gifted with a look of innocence—his expression is like that of a child opening presents—Brendan is a natural as the naive hero discovering the wonders of life. Like the characters he portrays in the films *Encino Man, George of the Jungle,* and *Blast from the Past,* Brendan is truly out of this world.

So You Want to Know—

How Brendan proposed to his wife? After five years of dating, Brendan and Afton were on vacation in Paris when Brendan took a photo of the two of them with his Polaroid camera. As Afton looked at the picture, she noticed Brendan was holding his jacket open despite the cold weather. At first Afton thought she was seeing a price tag inside the jacket, but she soon realized it was a note that read, "Will you marry me, Afton?"

Brendan Fraser
2118 Wilshire Blvd., #513
Santa Monica, CA 90403

Sarah Michelle Gellar

■ ■ ■ ■ ■ ■ ■ ■ ■ ■ ■ ■ ■

*A*n actress since age 4, Sarah Michelle is no stranger to the big or the small screen. The success of her TV show *Buffy the Vampire Slayer,* as well as a number of box office hits, has catapulted her to the forefront of stardom. She handles it all with grace and charm. "The funny thing is that when it happens to you, you don't really have time to stop and think about it. Your life changes very quickly and it's very hard to adapt to that change." Sarah Michelle has managed to juggle her TV work with her on-location movie shoots so well that her fans get a good dose of her all year round.

So You Want to Know—

Is all this popularity new to Sarah Michelle? She says it certainly is. Although she attended a private school in New York City, she was "the tortured scholarship child, the outcast who doesn't have the house in the Hamptons or the yacht or the nanny or the au pair." Despite this lack of popularity, or perhaps because of it, she blossomed into the sensitive young woman she is today.

Birthday Beat
April 14, 1977

Super Stats

➤ Birthplace: New York City
➤ Big break: discovered by a casting agent in New York City before she was 4
➤ Achievement: almost got a brown belt in Tae Kwon Do
➤ Hidden talent: Sarah once took a stab at competitive skating before she made it on the small screen.
➤ Likes: going to football and baseball games
➤ Dating: doesn't want to date someone in the industry because she doesn't think it's fair to him
➤ Collects: antique books
➤ Self-defined personality flaw: "I'm an amazing klutz."

Cool Credits

➤ TV: *Buffy the Vampire Slayer, All My Children,* the TV movie *A Woman Named Jackie*
➤ Won a 1994 Daytime Emmy for *All My Children*
➤ Film: *Funny Farm, High Stakes, Scream 2, I Know What You Did Last Summer, Simply Irresistible, Cruel Intentions*

Sarah Michelle Gellar
20th Century Fox Productions
10201 W. Pico Blvd.
Los Angeles, CA 90035

Tom Glavine

□ □ □ □ □ □ □ □ □ □ □ □ □ □ □ □ □ □ □

Although Tom was drafted by the Los Angeles Kings to play professional hockey, he chose baseball and signed with the Atlanta Braves instead. He certainly made a great choice. Tom went on to win the Cy Young Award for best pitcher in the National League after the 1998 season, just a few days after he got married. This is only a snapshot of the picture-perfect life that Tom has pitched for himself both on and off the mound. He believes that preparation is the key to success and practices this belief in his personal and professional life, which has made him a winner no matter what game he plays.

So You Want to Know—

How Tom prepares for a game? He chews on a piece of Bazooka sugarless bubble gum and keeps another piece in his back pocket when he pitches.

Super Stats

➤ Team: Atlanta Braves (pitcher)
➤ Height: 6'1"
➤ Weight: 185
➤ Birthplace: Concord, Massachusetts
➤ Strength: bats and throws left-handed
➤ Family: daughter, Amber Nicole; brother, Mike, first baseman for the Cleveland Indians
➤ Personal holiday: December 17, 1995, was Tom Glavine Day in his hometown of Billerica, Massachusetts.
➤ Personal possessions in his locker: pictures of his daughter, a framed four-leaf clover someone sent him, assorted baseball caps, a picture of the Blue Angels flight precision team, and a couple of hockey sticks

Cool Credits

➤ Named National League Pitcher of the Year by *The Sporting News*, 1991
➤ Named left-handed pitcher on *The Sporting News* National League All-Star Team, 1991, 1992, 1998
➤ Named pitcher on *The Sporting News* National League Silver Slugger team, 1991, 1995, 1996, 1998
➤ Named National League Cy Young Award winner by Baseball Writers' Association of America, 1991, 1998

Birthday Beat
March 23, 1966

Tom Glavine
c/o Atlanta Braves
P.O. Box 4064
Atlanta, GA 30302

Ken Griffey Jr.

▼▼▼▼▼▼▼▼▼▼▼▼▼▼▼▼▼▼

Ken Jr. has been one of the most consistently solid hitters since entering the major league in 1986. Son of the great Ken Griffey Sr., Ken Jr. is on his way to becoming one of the best in baseball history. He is already the second youngest player to reach 300 home runs and shares the major-league record for most consecutive games with one or more homers.

So You Want to Know—

Is Ken Jr. really a pop icon? Well, let's just say he has already reached a certain status. In 1989, a candy bar was named after him!

Super Stats

➤ Team: Seattle
Mariners (outfielder)
➤ Height: 6'3"
➤ Weight: 205
➤ Birthplace: Donora,
Pennsylvania
➤ Family: wife, Melissa;
son, Trey; brother, Craig,
outfielder for the Seattle
Mariners and Cincinnati
Reds (1991–97)

Cool Credits

➤ Selected by Seattle
Mariners in first round
(first pick overall) of free-
agent draft
➤ American League all-
star, 1990–98
➤ Career grand slams:
10
➤ American League
MVP, 1997
➤ Hit three home runs in
one game (May 24, 1996,
and April 25, 1997)
➤ Led American League
with 23 intentional bases
on balls, 1997
➤ Led American League
in slugging percentage
with .646, 1997

Birthday Beat

November 21, 1969

Ken Griffey Jr.
c/o Seattle Mariners
P.O. Box 4100
83 King St.
Seattle, WA 98104

Jennifer Love Hewitt

So You Want to Know—

What Jennifer does in her spare time? Jennifer is a self-described workaholic. She even works in her sleep! She literally dreamed up the concept of the film *Marry Me Jane,* about a wedding planner who falls for a client. She sold the idea, and you'll see her in the credits not only as the star, but also as executive producer.

Cool Credits

➤ TV: *Kids Incorporated, Shaky Ground, Party of Five, Time of Your Life*
➤ Film: *Munchies, Sister Act 2: Back in the Habit, House Arrest, I Know What You Did Last Summer, Can't Hardly Wait, I Still Know What You Did Last Summer, Marry Me Jane*
➤ Albums: *Love Songs, Let's Go Bang, Jennifer Love Hewitt*

Super Stats

➤ Height: 5'2½"
➤ Birthplace: Waco, Texas
➤ Current residence: the San Fernando Valley, California, with her mom, Pat
➤ Nickname: Love
➤ Fave foods: strawberries with whipped cream, Coke and Pepsi, mushroom pizza, and chocolate
➤ Best friend: her mom
➤ Hobby: arts and crafts—making fancy boxes and painting pottery, and giving them to her friends
➤ Fave groups: Smash Mouth, Third Eye Blind, Matchbox 20, Backstreet Boys, and 98 Degrees

No stranger to stage and screen, Jennifer was born to perform. When she was 3 years old, she managed to sneak away from her mom at a dinner club and soon was on stage singing! Within two years, she had already started dance lessons, and by the time she was 10, she was traveling around the world, performing in front of large audiences. Her secret? When she's working, she devotes "250,000 percent" to everything she does.

Birthday Beat
February 21, 1979

Jennifer Love Hewitt
c/o Party of Five
Fox Broadcasting Company
10201 W. Pico Blvd.
Los Angeles, CA 90035

Lauryn Hill

□ □ □ □ □ □ □ □ □ □ □ □ □ □ □ □ □ □ □

So You Want to Know—

What her album *The Miseducation of Lauryn Hill* is about? "The concept of *Miseducation* is not really miseducation at all," explains Lauryn. "To me, it's more or less switching the terminology. It's really about the things that you've learned outside of school, outside of what society deems appropriate and mandatory....There was a lot that I had to learn, 'life lessons,' that wasn't part of any scholastic curriculum."

Super Stats

➤ Current residence: lives in the house she was born and raised in, in South Orange, New Jersey
➤ Family: daughter, Selah Louise Hill
➤ How she's described: Public Enemy's Chuck D admiringly describes Lauryn as "sunlight" and a "Bob Marley [of the] 21st century"

Cool Credits

➤ TV: *As the World Turns, King of the Hill*
➤ Film: *Sister Act 2: Back in the Habit, Daddy's Girl, Hav Plenty, Rhyme and Reason, Restaurant*
➤ Hit songs: "You're Just Too Good to Be True," "Joyful Joyful"
➤ Debut album: *The Miseducation of Lauryn Hill*
➤ With the Fugees, won two 1996 Grammys: Best Rap Album for *The Score* and Best R&B Performance by a Duo or Group with Vocal

□ □ □ □ □ □ □ □ □ □ □ □ □ □ □ □ □ □ □

Having begun her career as an actress, Lauryn jumped into the music scene with her captivating vocals, both in a supporting role with the group the Fugees and as a solo artist. Lauryn has been described as confrontational, strong, forthright, and intelligent but with a delicate, sensitive temperament. She uses her music as a form of healing and a form of expression. "Every time I got hurt, every time I was disappointed, every time I learned, I just wrote a song."

Birthday Beat
May 26, 1975

Lauryn Hill
Sony Music
550 Madison Ave.
New York, NY 10022-3211
Official Web site: www.laurynhill.com

Martina Hingis

▼▼▼▼▼▼▼▼▼▼▼▼▼▼▼▼▼▼▼

Coached by her mother, Melanie Molitor, tennis phenom Martina turned pro just two weeks after her 14th birthday. Now, at 18, Martina has won more titles than many established players dream about. She has taken the tennis circuit by storm, skyrocketing to the No. 1 spot and renewing public interest in the game, as fans from around the world gather to see her play.

So You Want to Know—

Is Martina superstitious? Although she likes to hit the lines during a match, she will never walk on them, fearing it will bring bad luck.

Cool Credits

➤ Became the third woman in the Open Era to hold the No. 1 ranking in singles and doubles simultaneously, June 1997

➤ At age 16 years, 9 months, and 5 days, became the youngest player in the Open Era to win the singles title at Wimbledon, 1997

➤ First Swiss woman to win Wimbledon, 1997

Super Stats

➤ Height: 5'6"
➤ Birthplace: Kosice, Slovakia
➤ Current residence: Trübbach, Switzerland
➤ Enjoys: skiing, soccer, basketball, swimming, and horseback riding
➤ Owns: two horses, Montana and Sorrenta

➤ Martina's name: Her parents named her after tennis legend Martina Navratilova.

➤ Magazine cover: First female athlete to be on the cover of the men's magazine *GQ,* June 1998

➤ Fave cities to shop: Paris and New York City

➤ Immortalized in wax at the famous Madame Tussaud's Wax Museum in London

➤ Fave musicals: *Miss Saigon* and *Lion King*

➤ Fave designers: Versace, Armani, and Donna Karan

Birthday Beat
September 30, 1980

Martina Hingis
Seidenbaum
CH-9477 Trübbach
Switzerland

Katie Holmes

Not quite your average girl next door (though many boys wish she was), Katie thought it wouldn't be possible for a Midwestern girl's acting career to take off. While visiting New York City, she attended an International Modeling and Talent Association convention, where she was discovered by an agent. She aced her first professional film audition and got a role in the acclaimed film *The Ice Storm*. From there she catapulted to stardom and landed her most well-known role as Joey on *Dawson's Creek*.

So You Want to Know—

Is Katie anything like Joey, the character she plays on *Dawson's Creek*? "Joey isn't the girl who gets all the guys. I wasn't like that either, so I can relate," says Katie. "I'm a small-town girl just like Joey. I was a little bit of a tomboy and also the youngest in my family, so I thought I knew everything. Like Joey, I made a lot of mistakes, but fortunately I haven't had the tragedy that she's experienced in her life."

Cool Credits

➤ TV: *Dawson's Creek*
➤ Named on *Entertainment Weekly*'s 1998 "It" List
➤ One of *Seventeen*'s Ten Most Beautiful People, June 1998
➤ Film: *The Ice Storm, Disturbing Behavior, Go, Killing Mrs. Tingle*

Super Stats

➤ Height: 5'8"
➤ Birthplace: Toledo, Ohio
➤ Current residence: Wilmington, North Carolina
➤ Family: is the youngest of three sisters
➤ Fave food: Jelly Bellies
➤ Fave drink: can't start the day without a Starbucks vanilla latte
➤ Fave actor: Tom Hanks
➤ Fave actresses: Jodie Foster, Meg Ryan
➤ Fave directors: Woody Allen, Ron Howard
➤ Fave movie: *My Best Friend's Wedding*
➤ Fave pastimes: dancing, running, watching movies, reading, listening to music

Katie Holmes
c/o *Dawson's Creek*
WB Network
4000 Warner Blvd.
Burbank, CA 91522

Allen Iverson

□ ◁

I n 1996, Allen elected to leave college to play pro basketball. He was drafted by the Philadelphia 76ers, the team he most wanted to play for, after he visited their facilities. The road wasn't an easy one for Allen, who avoided a 15-year jail sentence following a brawl at a bowling alley, then had to deal with negative publicity from the incident. Allen "rebounded," already breaking NBA records.

So You Want to Know—

Did Allen always want to play basketball? "Football was my first love. Still is. I didn't even want to play basketball at first. I thought it was soft. My mother's the one who made me go to tryouts. I'll thank her forever. I came back and said: 'I like basketball, too.'"

Cool Credits

➤ Was the first 76er to win the 1996–97 Schick NBA Rookie of the Year Award, and named to the 1996–97 NBA All-Rookie First Team

➤ Selected by the 76ers with the first overall pick in the 1996 NBA draft

➤ Led the 76ers in 1996–97 in scoring (23.5 ppg, 6th in the NBA), assists (7.5 apg, 11th), and steals (2.07 spg, 7th) and set the Sixers' all-time rookie record with 1,787 points

➤ Led the 76ers in 1997–98 in scoring (22.0 ppg, 8th in the NBA), assists (6.2 apg, 16th), and steals (2.20 spg, 5th)

➤ Scored a 1997–98 season-high 43 points and grabbed 4 rebounds against the Minnesota Timberwolves on April 10, 1998

Super Stats

➤ Team: Philadelphia 76ers
➤ Height: 6'
➤ Weight: 165
➤ Birthplace: Hampton, Virginia
➤ Hobby: drawing
➤ Fave book: *The Color Purple*
➤ Family: daughter, Tiaura; son, Allen II
➤ Fun fact: At age 15, he dunked in a game for the first time.

Birthday Beat
June 7, 1975

Allen Iverson
c/o Philadelphia 76ers
Veterans Stadium
P.O. Box 25040
Philadelphia, PA 19147-0240

Jewel

▼▼▼▼▼▼▼▼▼▼▼▼▼▼▼▼▼▼▼▼▼

Growing up in Alaska on an 800-acre plot of land in a house with no running water or television, Jewel helped tend her family's garden and take care of their horses. Her parents were a singing/songwriting duo, and by the time she was 6, Jewel was traveling around Alaska, performing with them. When her parents split, she stayed with her father until she was a teenager, singing in bars and small venues throughout the state. Jewel received her most precious gift from her mother, who taught her about music, art, and poetry from an early age.

Birthday Beat
May 23, 1974

44

Super Stats
➤ Full name: Jewel Kilcher
➤ Birthplace: Homer, Alaska

➤ Education: Interlochen Arts Academy, Michigan
➤ Studied: opera, sculpture, dance, and drama when she was in high school
➤ Never leaves home without it: a Tupperware container of genuine Homer, Alaska, soil wherever she goes on tour so that she'll never be far from her roots

Cool Credits

➤ Albums: *Pieces of You, Spirit*
➤ Book: *Night Without Armor,* a collection of poetry
➤ Film: *Ride with the Devil*
➤ Won the American Music Award for Best New Artist

So You Want to Know—

Has Jewel's road to success been easy? Not at all. At 17, she moved to San Diego to live with her mother. After a few unsuccessful jobs, she decided to live in her van and write songs. She spent her days in coffeehouses writing poetry and eating little more than peanut butter and carrots. Fortunately, it wasn't long before she was offered a regular gig at a coffeehouse, and her career grew from there.

Jewel
P.O. Box 33494
San Diego, CA 92163-3494
Official Web site: jeweljk.com

Jason Kidd

■ ■ ■ ■ ■ ■ ■ ■ ■ ■ ■ ■ ■ ■ ■

*T*outed as the next Magic Johnson, Jason left college early and was picked No. 2 in the NBA draft by the Dallas Mavericks. He now plays for the Phoenix Suns and has reached superstar status, electrifying his fans with precision passing and shooting night after night. Among the very best in the NBA, Kidd is no longer a kid.

So You Want to Know—

Is basketball the only sport Jason follows? Not at all. Jason follows baseball very closely and is a devoted collector of baseball memorabilia. One of his most prized possessions is a bat autographed by Ken Griffey Jr.

Cool Credits

➤ NBA co-Rookie of the Year, 1995; NBA All-Rookie First Team, 1995
➤ Named to the NBA All-Defensive First Team, 1998, 1999
➤ Led the NBA in assists (10.8 apg) and triple-doubles (7), and also led the Suns in double-doubles (30, 3rd in the NBA) and steals (2.28 spg, 4th), 1998, 1999
➤ Named NBA Player of the Month for April 1999, averaging 20.1 ppg, 10.4 apg, 6.7 rpg, and 2.38 spg, and logging two triple-doubles, for the Suns

Birthday Beat
March 23, 1973

➤ Scored his 4,000th career point and logged a triple-double, with 14 points and game-highs of 16 assists and 12 rebounds, in a 94–86 win over the Vancouver Grizzlies on February 25, 1999

Super Stats

➤ Team: Phoenix Suns
➤ Height: 6'4"
➤ Weight: 212
➤ Hobby: playing video games
➤ Personal goal: hitting a hole-in-one
➤ Charity: Each Thanksgiving he and other San Francisco Bay Area native NBA players feed several thousand homeless people.
➤ Fave music: R&B
➤ Fave performers: Chante Moore and the Isley Brothers

Jason Kidd
c/o Phoenix Suns
P.O. Box 1369
Phoenix, AZ 85001

Michelle Kwan

*A*fter watching her brother play hockey, Michelle decided to learn how to skate. By the time she was 13, she had conquered the world of ice skating. Having matured in a short period of time from a "pony-tailed little girl" into the graceful young woman who won the World Championships and a silver medal at the 1998 Olympics, Michelle is well on her way to winning the Olympic gold.

Birthday Beat
July 7, 1980

□ □ □ □ □ □ □ □ □ □ □ □ □ □ □ □ □

Super Stats

➤ Height: 5'3"
➤ Birthplace and current residence: Torrance, California
➤ Nickname: Shelly
➤ Family: has an older sister, Karen, who also skates
➤ Fab feat: landed six triple jumps at the 1993 Olympic Festival

Cool Credits

➤ At 12 years of age, finished sixth at the National Championships
➤ Silver medal at U.S. Championships, 1995, 1996
➤ Gold medal at World Championships, 1996, 1998
➤ Silver medal at World Championships, 1997
➤ Olympic silver medalist, 1998
➤ National Champion, 1998, 1999

So You Want to Know—

Does Michelle have a mischievous side? In 1992, Michelle finished in ninth place at the Junior Championships but wanted to take the test for the senior level. Her coach didn't think she was ready. Michelle waited until her coach was out of town and had her parents, who thought the coach knew about it, take her to the test. Oh, by the way, she passed with flying colors!

Michelle Kwan
c/o Ice Castle
P.O. Box 939480
Cottage Grove Rd.
Lake Arrowhead, CA 92352

Jake Lloyd

▼▼▼▼▼▼▼▼▼▼▼▼▼▼▼▼▼▼▼▼▼▼▼

Jake knew he wanted to be an actor the first time he saw *Terminator 2: Judgment Day,* and he began telling everyone he was Arnold Schwarzenegger. Ironically, he ended up playing Arnold's son in the movie *Jingle All the Way.* Although Jake is young, he has already built a solid career as an actor, landing the role of Anakin Skywalker in the blockbuster *Star Wars* movie *The Phantom Menace.* When Jake was 5 years old, he dressed up as Darth Vader for Halloween. A year later, he was selected out of 3,000 contestants for the role of young Anakin. "If Jake wants it, he gets it," says his father. Although he loves acting, Jake still finds time to have fun and be a kid, enjoying baseball, video games, and Rollerblading.

Birthday Beat
March 5, 1989

Cool Credits

➤ Film: *Unhook the Stars, Jingle All the Way, Star Wars Episode I: The Phantom Menace*
➤ TV appearances: *ER*, and a recurring role on *The Pretender*

So You Want to Know—

What Jake will wear next Halloween? Jake is prepared: He was given his Anakin Skywalker costume as a souvenir. "It's the last costume I wore in the film," he says. He's just worried that by the time Halloween comes around, he may not fit into it anymore!

Super Stats

➤ Birthplace: Fort Collins, Colorado
➤ Current residence: southern California
➤ Family: mother, Lisa, is a theatrical agent; father, Bill, is an emergency medical technician who works on film sets; sister, Madison, is also an actor
➤ Fave subject: science
➤ Stars he'd like to meet: Will Smith, Harrison Ford, Mark Hamill
➤ Pet peeve: people who smoke
➤ Future goal: to put all the money he makes from acting toward his future, including college
➤ Pet: a dog, J.J.
➤ Fun fact: plays outfield on his Little League team

Jake Lloyd
c/o Osbrink Talent Agency
4605 Lankershim Blvd., #408
North Hollywood, CA 91602

Rebecca Lobo

▪ ▪ ▪ ▪ ▪ ▪ ▪ ▪ ▪ ▪ ▪ ▪ ▪ ▪ ▪ ▪

Both on and off the basketball court, Rebecca has always been at the top of her game. She made the dean's list every semester in college and was first team Academic All America, while breaking basketball records and establishing herself as one of the most dominant players in women's basketball history.

So You Want to Know—

What historical figures Rebecca would want to invite to a dinner party? Thomas Jefferson, because "he was a renaissance man"; David Robinson, who is her basketball hero; Bruce Springsteen, whom she idolizes; Robin Williams, for his jokes; and Julia Child. Why Julia? "I'm not cooking for this shindig," Rebecca says with a smile.

Birthday Beat
October 6, 1973

Super Stats

➤ Team: New York Liberty
➤ Height: 6'4"
➤ College: University of Connecticut
➤ Degree: political science
➤ Writing credit: co-wrote a daughter-mother autobiography called *The Home Team* in 1996
➤ Fave charity: organizations that support breast cancer research and awareness, due to her mother's battle with the disease
➤ Fun fact: jogged with President Bill Clinton during a visit to the White House
➤ Pastimes: reading John Grisham novels and watching Roadrunner cartoons

Cool Credits

➤ Reached the WNBA Championship game with the New York Liberty, 1997
➤ Named to the All-WNBA Second Team, 1997
➤ Won 102 consecutive games starting in college up until joining the Liberty
➤ Youngest member of the U.S. Women's Olympic Team that won the gold medal at the 1996 Atlanta Games
➤ Member of the undefeated U.S. Women's Basketball National Team, 1996
➤ Led UConn to a 35–0 record and the NCAA Championship and was named Final Four MVP, 1995

Rebecca Lobo
New York Liberty
Two Penn Plaza
New York, NY 10121

Ricky Martin

Blessed with charisma, charm, and multicultural appeal, Ricky is refreshingly humble about his success and grateful that hard work, talent, and fortune have taken him so far. From school plays to TV commercials to his musical debut in the group Menudo at age 12, Ricky has grown up with music and performing as core themes in his life. A believer in destiny, he puts equal faith in being prepared and having a positive attitude. "Everything I've accomplished is because I've been ready for it," says Ricky. "Planning, discipline, and a good outlook are the keys to success."

Birthday Beat

December 24, 1971

Cool Credits

➤ Was in pop group Menudo
➤ TV: *General Hospital*
➤ Broadway: *Les Misérables*

➤ Won 1999 Grammy for Best Latin Pop Performance for his album *Vuelve*

So You Want to Know—

Would Ricky ever give up performing? He says music is a way of life and wants to keep doing it until the day he dies. But if he ever gets tired of singing, he has no problem moving on to something else. "Life is too short to be doing something you don't like, so let's take advantage of every moment."

Super Stats

➤ Full name: Enrique Martin Morales
➤ Birthplace: Hato Rey, Puerto Rico
➤ Family: father is a psychologist; mother is an accountant; siblings Fernando, Angel, Eric, Daniel, and Vanessa
➤ Inspirations: Daniel Day-Lewis, Sting, Barbra Streisand
➤ Fave food: Italian
➤ Least fave food: seafood
➤ Music influences: Boston, Cheap Trick
➤ Fave type of books: poetry, philosophy, art, and the classics
➤ Biggest fear: snakes
➤ What makes him angry: lying
➤ Smartest thing he ever did: get involved in the music business

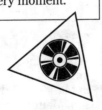

Ricky Martin
c/o Columbia Records
550 Madison Ave.
New York, NY 10022

Mark McGwire

Cool Credits

➤ College Player of the Year, 1984
➤ Played on the U.S. Olympic team, 1984
➤ Selected by the Oakland A's in first round in 1984 draft
➤ Rookie of the Year, 1987
➤ Set a record for home runs by a rookie: 49, 1987
➤ Led American League in home runs, 1987, 1996
➤ Won World Series for the A's, 1989
➤ American League All-Star, 1987–92, 1995–97
➤ First to hit more than 50 home runs in consecutive seasons, 1996–98
➤ Led the majors in home runs: 58, 1997
➤ *Sporting News* Man of the Year, 1997
➤ Led the majors in home runs: 70, 1998

Super Stats

➤ Team: St. Louis Cardinals
➤ Height: 6'5"
➤ Birthplace: Pomona, California
➤ Current residence: Long Beach, California
➤ Family: son, Matthew; brother, Dan, played in the NFL for the Miami Dolphins and the Seattle Seahawks
➤ Charity: started the Mark McGwire Foundation in 1997 to help abused children and plans to donate $1 million to it each season
➤ Education: attended USC

So You Want to Know—

Who the most important person is in Mark's life? His son, Matthew, who was in attendance when his dad broke the record for most home runs in a single season.

Bursting into the major leagues in 1987, Mark is one of the most dominant home-run hitters in baseball. Opposing pitchers get the chills whenever Mark steps up to the plate, dwarfing the batter's box with his incredibly large stature. In 1998, he sparked a resurgence of interest in pro baseball by shattering the long-standing home-run record of 61 set by Roger Maris in 1961, and went on to hit a mind-boggling 70 homers. Mark is a symbol of success to baseball fans around the world.

Birthday Beat
October 1, 1963

Mark McGwire
c/o St. Louis Cardinals
250 Stadium Plaza
St. Louis, MO 63102

Alyssa Milano

▪ ▪ ▪ ▪ ▪ ▪ ▪ ▪ ▪ ▪ ▪ ▪ ▪ ▪ ▪

Despite having appeared in almost 20 films, until just a couple of years ago Alyssa was best known for her long-standing TV role as Samantha Micelli on *Who's the Boss*. Viewers were skeptical when she appeared on the hit TV drama *Melrose Place,* but right from the start it was crystal clear that little Alyssa had grown up. She currently stars as one of three sisters gifted with supernatural powers on the TV series *Charmed*.

So You Want to Know—

If it's hard for Alyssa to be in the public eye all the time? Alyssa loves her fans, but some of them have taken advantage of her by posting naked pictures of her on the Internet without her knowledge. When she found out about it, she was horrified. She took action and successfully sued the culprits. Alyssa considers her win a victory for celebrities everywhere.

Cool Credits

➤ Broadway: *Annie*
➤ Won three Youth in Film awards for Best Supporting Actress for *Who's the Boss*
➤ TV: *Who's the Boss, Melrose Place, Charmed;* appeared on *The Outer Limits, Spin City, Fantasy Island, Total Request with Carson Daly;* played Amy Fisher in the TV movie *Casualties of Love: The Long Island Lolita Story*
➤ Film: *Commando, The Canterville Ghost, Speed Zone!, Where the Day Takes You, Double Dragon, Poison Ivy II, Fear, Glory Daze, Below Utopia, Jimmy Zip*

Super Stats

➤ Full name: Alyssa Jayne Milano
➤ Height: 5'2 "
➤ Birthplace: Brooklyn, New York
➤ Family: younger brother, Corey, also an actor; mother, Lin, a fashion designer; father, Tom, a music editor; husband, Cinjun Tate, is the lead singer for the rock group Remy Zero
➤ Nicknames: Lyssa, Conan
➤ Fave place: Disneyland
➤ Musical talents: plays piano and flute
➤ Pets: three dogs, Ripley, Stella, and Hugo

Birthday Beat
December 19, 1972

Alyssa Milano
c/o United Talent Agency
9560 Wilshire Blvd., Suite 500
Beverly Hills, CA 90212

'N Sync

□ □ □ □ □ □ □ □ □ □ □ □ □ □ □ □ □

J.C. Chasez and Justin Timberlake met way back when they were starring on *The New Mickey Mouse Club*. Both traveled to Nashville, Tennessee, where they worked with the same vocal coach. Justin later met up with Joey Fatone, Chris Allen, and Lance Buss, and they decided to form a group. They invited J.C. to join them, and 'N Sync was born.

Their first album was released in Munich, Germany, but their music caught on all across Europe. Word spread about these cool kids, and they exploded onto the music scene back home in the United States. These days, fans just can't get enough of these five hot stars!

Birthday Beat

J.C.: August 8, 1976
Justin: January 31, 1981
Joey: January 28, 1977
Lance: May 4, 1979
Chris: October 17, 1971

Cool Credits

➤ TV appearance: *Sabrina the Teenage Witch*
➤ Albums: *'N Sync, Home for Christmas, Winter Album*
➤ Film: performed songs on the soundtrack for Disney's *Tarzan* with Phil Collins

So You Want to Know—

How 'N Sync feels about their newfound fame? "We're kids from the suburbs and we're singing about having a good time," says Chris, "because we want to have a good time and we want everyone with us to have a good time."

Super Stats

➤ Full names: J.C.—Joshua Scott Chasez; Joey—Joseph Anthony Fatone Jr.; Chris—Christopher Allen Kirkpatrick; Lance—James Lance Bass; Justin—Justin Timberlake
➤ Fave foods: Justin—cereal; Chris—Mexican; Joey—Italian; J.C.—Chinese; Lance—French toast
➤ Band formed: Orlando, Florida, 1996
➤ Craziest thing to happen on stage: Justin slipped while dancing and broke his thumb—but he still finished singing the song!

'N Sync
c/o Wright Stuff Management
7380 St. Lake Rd., #350
Orlando, FL 32819
Official Web site: www.nsync.com

98 Degrees

▼▼▼▼▼▼▼▼▼▼▼▼▼▼▼▼▼▼▼▼▼▼▼

Jeff Timmons, the founding member of 98 Degrees, was studying psychology at Kent State University when he decided to move to Los Angeles to pursue a career in music and acting. He put together a few bands, but none seemed quite right until 1994, when a friend introduced him to Nick Lachey, who brought in his brother, Drew, and friend Justin Jeffre. After a few unsuccessful attempts auditioning for an L.A. Dodgers game, the boys resorted to singing in the lobby of the team's corporate offices. When the halls quickly filled up with excited listeners, the execs responded. After being together only one week, 98 Degrees played to a packed house at a Dodgers/Cincinnati Reds game.

Birthday Beat

Jeff: April 30, 1973
Nick: November 9, 1973
Drew: August 8, 1976
Justin: February 25, 1973

▼▼▼▼▼▼▼▼▼▼▼▼▼▼▼▼▼▼

Cool Credits

➤ Albums: *98 Degrees, 98 Degrees and Rising*
➤ Singles: "True to Your Heart" with Stevie Wonder for Disney's hit film *Mulan,* "Invisible Man," and "Because of You"
➤ Tours: 1999 All That Music and More Tour with Monica, B*Witched, Tatyana Ali, and Aaron Carter

Super Stats

➤ Heights: Jeff—5'8"; Nick—5'11"; Justin—5'10"; Drew—5'6"
➤ Nicknames: Nick—Hollywood, Slider; Jeff—Sugar; Drew—Sprout; Justin—Droopy, Big J, Hydro
➤ Birthplaces: Nick—Harlan, Kentucky; Drew—Cincinnati, Ohio; Justin—Mount Clemens, Michigan; Jeff—Canton, Ohio

So You Want to Know—

What's next for 98 Degrees? They want to be seen as a respected group, not just as a "boy band." As Jeff says, "There are some things we want to accomplish...not only the attainable goals like physical things like Grammys and number one songs or things like that, but I think we just want to expand artistically, to sing with other artists, rock groups, things like that."

• •

98 Degrees
c/o Motown
825 Eighth Ave., 29th Floor
New York, NY 10019

• •

Rosie O'Donnell

■ ■ ■ ■ ■ ■ ■ ■ ■ ■ ■ ■ ■ ■ ■ ■ ■ ■

Being the middle child in a family of five, Rosie could have gotten lost in the shuffle. Instead, it gave her an opportunity to excel. She loved sports and played almost all of them. When Rosie was 10, her mother died. She still managed to keep her grades up, and graduated as both senior class president *and* prom queen. Rosie began doing stand-up comedy when she was 17 and was a five-time winner on *Star Search*. Her career took Rosie into television, film, TV commercials, and now her own top-rated talk show.

So You Want to Know—

How did the *Rosie O'Donnell Show* come about? Soon after she adopted her son, Rosie wanted to give up films so she could spend more time at home. She came up with the idea of a talk show. Within its first four months, the *Rosie O'Donnell Show* was ranked the No. 1 daytime talk show.

Cool Credits

➤ Film: *A League of Their Own, Sleepless in Seattle, Another Stakeout, I'll Do Anything, The Flintstones, Exit to Eden, Now and Then, Beautiful Girls, Harriet the Spy, Tarzan*
➤ Hosted the 1998–99 Kids Choice Awards
➤ TV: *Rosie O'Donnell Show, Gimme a Break, Stand By Your Man, Twilight of the Golds*
➤ Hosted *Stand-Up Spotlight* on VH-1
➤ Won a Kids Choice Award for Best Actress, *Harriet the Spy*
➤ Broadway: *Grease*
➤ Won two 1998 Emmy Awards for Best Talk Show and Best Talk Show Host
➤ Hosted the 1998 Tony Awards

Super Stats

➤ Full name: Roseanna O'Donnell
➤ Birthplace: Commack, New York
➤ Background: grew up mostly on Long Island, New York, but spent some time in Ireland after her mother died
➤ Family: adopted son, Parker; adopted daughter, Chelsea Belle
➤ Collects: toys, especially those in McDonald's Happy Meals
➤ Role models: Barbra Streisand, Bette Midler
➤ Star buddy: best friends with Madonna

Birthday Beat
March 21, 1962

Rosie O'Donnell
30 Rockefeller Plaza, #800E
New York, NY 10112
Official Web site: rosieo.warnerbros.com

Shaquille O'Neal

□ □ □ □ □ □ □ □ □ □ □ □ □ □ □ □ □ □

After seeing pictures of Shaq lifting up fellow hoopsters Magic Johnson and Hakeem Olajuwon, it's obvious to see how powerful a physical presence he can be to opposing players. Shaq burst onto the professional basketball scene at age 20, playing for the Orlando Magic. In six years with the NBA, he has played in the NBA finals with Orlando and set numerous basketball records, not to mention leading the sagging Los Angeles Lakers in a mighty revival. Shaq's on-court presence translates surprisingly well to off-court stardom. He has made quite a name for himself as both a rap star and movie star.

So You Want to Know—

Does Shaquille do more than slam-dunk? As Shaq-a-Claus, he purchased toys to distribute at Christmas to disadvantaged central Florida youths, and also dressed up as Shaq-a-Bunny for Easter.

Cool Credits

➤ Five rap albums: *Shaq Diesel, Shaq Fu: Da Return, You Can't Stop the Reign, Respect,* and a greatest hits album

➤ Owns a record label and clothing line called TWIsM

➤ Film: *Kazaam, Blue Chips, He Got Game*

➤ Led the NBA in field-goal percentage (.576) and also led the Lakers in scoring (26.3, 2nd), rebounds (10.7 rpg, 7th), and blocked shots (1.67 bpg, 14th)

➤ Member of gold medal–winning U.S. Olympic Team, 1996

Super Stats

➤ Team: Los Angeles Lakers (center)

➤ Height: 7'1"

➤ Weight: 315

➤ Shoe size: 22

➤ Full name: Shaquille Rashaun O'Neal

➤ Origin: his name, Shaquille Rashaun, means "little warrior"

➤ Education: attended Louisiana State University

➤ Fave animal: his dog, Thor, a 130-pound rottweiler

➤ Food he grew up eating: army food and fast food

➤ Fave singers: Guy, TLC, K-Ci & Jojo and Laccord

Birthday Beat

March 6, 1972

Shaquille O'Neal
c/o Los Angeles Lakers
3900 W. Manchester Blvd.
P.O. Box 10
Inglewood, CA 90306
Official Web site: www.shaq.com

Gwyneth Paltrow

Super Stats

➤ Full name: Gwyneth Kate Paltrow
➤ Height: 5'9"
➤ Birthplace: Los Angeles, California
➤ Raised in: New York and Massachusetts
➤ Language: speaks fluent Spanish
➤ Education: attended University of California, Santa Barbara, and majored in art history but quit to pursue acting
➤ Fave movie: *There's Something About Mary*
➤ Hobbies: reading, watching football, cooking, going to bookstores, and spending time with friends

Cool Credits

➤ Film: *Flesh and Bone, Hush, A Perfect Murder, Great Expectations, Out of the Past, Sliding Doors, Shakespeare in Love, The Pallbearer, Emma, Hard Eight, Jefferson in Paris, Higher Learning, Moonlight and Valentino, Seven*
➤ Won the 1998 Golden Globe for Best Actress in a Musical or Comedy, *Shakespeare in Love*
➤ Won the 1998 Academy Award for Best Actress, *Shakespeare in Love*
➤ One of *People* magazine's 50 Most Beautiful People, 1998

Birthday Beat

September 28, 1973

So You Want to Know—

If being a great performer is in the genes? Gwyneth is the daughter of award-winning actress Blythe Danner and TV producer Bruce Paltrow, and is the sister of actor Jake Paltrow.

Despite her delicate beauty, Gwyneth has a strong presence both on stage and in person. Though she had appeared in three previous films, her star quality first surfaced in *Flesh and Bone* in 1993 with James Caan and Dennis Quaid. Gwyneth's sparkle was not diminished by the power and intensity of her co-stars. Her poise and grace shined through and propelled her into a variety of roles. With

her versatility, talent, and a brand-new Oscar for Best Actress, Gwyneth will go far in the acting world.

• •

Gwyneth Paltrow
c/o CAA
9830 Wilshire Blvd.
Beverly Hills, CA 90212

• •

Natalie Portman

■ ■ ■ ■ ■ ■ ■ ■ ■ ■ ■ ■ ■ ■ ■

Discovered at a pizza parlor when she was 11, Natalie exudes a charm and maturity that are impossible to ignore. Natalie began her career as a model and was cast in a starring role in *The Professional* when she was only 13. She has since appeared on Broadway and in numerous films, lending her remarkable talent to each role she portrays. On screen and off, Natalie is a natural. Perhaps that is the quality that prompted director George Lucas to cast her as Queen Amidala in the *Star Wars* film *The Phantom Menace*. Natalie is protective of her private life, and her fans seem willing to give her the space she needs to grow and develop as an actress and as an individual.

Cool Credits

➤ Broadway: Anne in *The Diary of Anne Frank*
➤ Film: *The Professional, Where the Heart Is, Anywhere But Here, Star Wars Episode I: The Phantom Menace, The Prince of Egypt, Mars Attacks!, Beautiful Girls, Everyone Says I Love You, Heat*

Super Stats

➤ Height: 5'4"
➤ Birthplace: Jerusalem, Israel
➤ Current residence: Long Island, New York
➤ Pastimes: reading, writing
➤ Siblings: none
➤ Fave food: chocolate
➤ Education: attended Stagedoor Manor Performing Arts Camp, 1994, 1995

So You Want to Know—

How Natalie felt about being cast in a *Star Wars* movie? When she was asked to try out for the part, Natalie recalls, "They said they were doing a new *Star Wars,* and I was like, yeah, OK, whatever." In fact, she had never seen any of the *Star Wars* movies! Despite the 10-year, three-film contract, and faced with the prospect of becoming almost too famous for her liking, Natalie decided to take the role, saying: "You know what? This is gonna be *fun*!"

Natalie Portman
International Creative Management
8942 Wilshire Blvd.
Beverly Hills, CA 90211

Freddie Prinze Jr.

□ □ □ □ □ □ □ □ □ □ □ □ □ □ □ □ □ □ □

*S*on of actor/comedian Freddie Prinze, handsome heartthrob Freddie Jr. bounced around to three different high schools before finally graduating. He then moved to Hollywood to pursue a career in acting and was immediately cast in a small role on the hit TV show *Family Matters*. From there his roles grew more significant. In the past three years, Freddie has appeared in seven feature films and has elevated himself to superstar status.

So You Want to Know—

What inspires Freddie to succeed as an actor? Freddie's father committed suicide in 1977 after his TV show, *Chico and the Man,* was canceled. His father's death affected him deeply. Freddie is determined to pay tribute by carrying on his dad's dream of success. He states, "It left a lot of open-ended questions to a son who had a lot of questions that needed to be answered. To an extent, it inspires you to want to succeed and do well, not only for your own sake, but to make your father proud."

Super Stats

➤ Height: 6'1"
➤ Birthplace: Albuquerque, New Mexico
➤ Fun fact: Freddie is left-handed.
➤ Fave food: Japanese. He claims he could eat it every day and never get sick of it.
➤ Hobby: recently took up tap dancing and believes it's a great way to express himself

Cool Credits

➤ Film: *She's All That, Wing Commander, I Still Know What You Did Last Summer, The House of Yes, To Gillian on Her 37th Birthday*
➤ TV: *Family Matters*

Birthday Beat
March 8, 1976

Freddie Prinze Jr.
c/o CAA
9830 Wilshire Blvd.
Beverly Hills, CA 90212

Keri Russell

▼▼▼▼▼▼▼▼▼▼▼▼▼▼▼▼▼▼▼

While modeling in Denver, Keri was discovered by Disney in a national talent search and landed her first role, in the film *Honey, I Blew Up the Kid.* Shortly thereafter, she was cast in *The New Mickey Mouse Club* and had to move from her home in Denver to Orlando, Florida. As soon as that stint ended, Keri packed up and moved to Los Angeles, where she landed a number of guest roles on TV shows. It wasn't until 1998 that Keri achieved true fame in her leading role as the enchanting Felicity, for which she has earned a Golden Globe.

So You Want to Know—

How Keri reacted to winning the Golden Globe? Keri doesn't take it all too seriously. "If you win a Golden Globe," she says, "no one's saying, 'You're a great person.' They're saying, 'We like purple and you're purple. Next week we'll like green.'"

Cool Credits

➤ Won the 1998 Golden Globe Award for Best Performance in a Television Drama
➤ Film: *Mad About Mambo, Dead Man's Curve, When Innocence Is Lost, Eight Days a Week, The Babysitter's Seduction, The Lottery, Honey, I Blew Up the Kid*
➤ TV: a regular on *The New Mickey Mouse Club, Emerald Cove, Daddy's Girls, Malibu Shores, Roar, Felicity*; appeared on *Married With Children, 7th Heaven, Boy Meets World*
➤ Starred in Bon Jovi's music video "Always"

Super Stats

➤ Full name: Keri Lynn Russell
➤ Height: 5'3"
➤ Birthplace: Fountain Valley, California
➤ Grew up in: Dallas, Texas; Mesa, Arizona; and Denver
➤ Origin: named after her grandfather Kermit
➤ Nickname: Care Bear
➤ Biggest passion: ballet, jazz, lyrical, and street dancing
➤ Pet: a cat, Nala
➤ Fave pastime: attending rock concerts
➤ Fave book: *Reviving Ophelia* by Mary Pipher
➤ Fun fact: Keri was kicked out of the Brownie Girl Scouts (for doing "too many cartwheels")

Birthday Beat

March 23, 1976

Keri Russell
c/o The Gersh Agency
232 N. Canon Dr.
Beverly Hills, CA 90210

Adam Sandler

Cool Credits

➤ Film: *Big Daddy, Little Nicky, Dirty Work, The Waterboy* (also executive producer, screenwriter), *The Wedding Singer, Bulletproof, Happy Gilmore* (also screenwriter), *Billy Madison* (also screenwriter), *Mixed Nuts, Airheads, Coneheads*

➤ Nominated for a Grammy for his debut comedy album, *They're All Gonna Laugh at You*

➤ TV: *The Cosby Show, Saturday Night Live, Remote Control*

Birthday Beat
September 9, 1966

Super Stats

➤ Birthplace: Brooklyn, New York
➤ Raised in: New Hampshire
➤ College: graduated from NYU with a degree in fine arts

So You Want to Know—

How Adam got his start? He was performing at the Improv in Los Angeles when Dennis Miller, an alumnus of *Saturday Night Live,* caught his act and recommended him to *SNL* producer Lorne Michaels. Adam was quickly hired as a writer and cast member, and a year later he had captured the hearts of TV viewers with his "Opera Man" and "Canteen Boy" characters.

From his earliest days, Adam never wanted to be anything but a comedian. He was a class clown starting in grammar school, and attended college while juggling a stand-up comedy career. In his freshman year, he had a recurring role on *The Cosby Show,* playing Theo's pal Smitty. His credentials also include writing and producing, and with box office hits like *The Wedding Singer* and *The Waterboy* under his belt, there's no stopping this wild and crazy guy!

Adam Sandler
5420 Worster Ave.
Van Nuys, CA 91401

Will Smith

Will and his junior high buddy Jeff rapped their way to musical stardom as D.J. Jazzy Jeff and the Fresh Prince. After achieving TV fame on *The Fresh Prince of Bel Air,* Will decided to end the show to pursue a film career. With star turns in the blockbusters *Independence Day* and *Men in Black,* Will has made a name for himself as a bona fide action-adventure hero, and has continued to crank out hit albums as well. Who knows what he'll try his hand at next?

Birthday Beat
September 25, 1969

Cool Credits

➤ Film: *Wild Wild West, Enemy of the State, Men in Black, Independence Day, Bad Boys, Made in America, Six Degrees of Separation, Where the Day Takes You, The Imagemaker*

➤ Albums: *Wild Wild West; Big Willie Style; Boom Shake the Room; Summertime; He's the D.J., I'm the Rapper; D.J. Jazzy Jeff and the Fresh Prince*

Super Stats

➤ Birthplace: Philadelphia, Pennsylvania (just like his character on *The Fresh Prince of Bel Air*)

➤ Current residence: Malibu, California

➤ Family: wife is actress Jada Pinkett Smith; sons, Jaden and Trey

➤ Fave cause: the "Stay in School" campaign (even though he turned down a scholarship to MIT to pursue his career)

So You Want to Know—

How strong and confident Will is? By the time he was 21, Will had made and lost a fortune due to bad management, but within a year he was back on his feet and going strong.

Will Smith
c/o Studio Fan Mail
1122 S. Robertson Blvd.
Los Angeles, CA 90035

Sammy Sosa

▼▼▼▼▼▼▼▼▼▼▼▼▼▼▼▼▼▼▼▼▼

S ammy has said numerous times, "Baseball has been very good to me." Well, it definitely has, but at the same time Sammy's been a great ambassador for the sport. His career and fame skyrocketed last year when he dueled with Mark McGwire for the home-run championship. Although being edged out, Sammy still finished the season as the National League MVP.

Birthday Beat
November 12, 1968

Cool Credits

➤ Named *Sports Illustrated*'s Co-Sportsman of the Year, 1998
➤ National League MVP and RBI leader, 1998
➤ Named Major League Player of the Year by *The Sporting News*, 1998
➤ Named National League MVP by Baseball Writers' Association of America, 1998
➤ Received the Gene Autry Courage Award for his generosity to children and the poor

Super Stats

➤ Team: Chicago Cubs (right fielder)
➤ Birthplace and current residence: San Pedro de Macoris, Dominican Republic
➤ Family: wife, Sonia; four children, Keysha, Kenia, Sammy Jr., and Michael; brother, Jose, played in the Cubs' minor league

So You Want to Know—

How long Sammy has been playing professional baseball? Some people think Sammy burst onto the scene in 1998 after his highly publicized home-run battle with Mark McGwire, but he's actually been playing pro baseball since 1986, when he was drafted by Texas's Gulf Coast (Rookie) club.

Sammy Sosa
c/o Chicago Cubs
1060 W. Addison St.
Chicago, IL 60613

Britney Spears

■ ■ ■ ■ ■ ■ ■ ■ ■ ■ ■ ■ ■ ■ ■ ■

Britney can't remember when she *didn't* want to be a singer. At age 8, she was turned down for *The New Mickey Mouse Club,* but the producer who recognized Britney's talent helped her get an agent. After appearing in commercials and off-Broadway shows, she finally landed a role on *The New Mickey Mouse Club.* After two years on the show, she went home to attend high school for one year, then she was back in the music spotlight. She's in love with performing and being on the road, but she always has a tutor travel with her to keep up her studies.

Birthday Beat

December 2, 1981

Cool Credits

➤ Was a member of The New Mickey Mouse Club
➤ Theater: appeared in *Ruthless,* an off-Broadway musical
➤ Album: *Baby One More Time*

Super Stats

➤ Birthplace: Kentwood, Louisiana
➤ Current residence: Kentwood, Louisiana, and New York City
➤ Family: parents, Jamie and Lynn; siblings, Bryan and Jamie Lynn
➤ Car: a Mercedes convertible
➤ Fave color: baby blue, because it's soft, pure, and sweet
➤ Loves: eating ice cream before going to bed, and pasta and baked potatoes covered with everything

➤ Fave cities: Chicago and Los Angeles
➤ Fave stores: Sugar Magnolia in Chicago, Abercrombie and Fitch
➤ Musical influences: Whitney Houston, Mariah Carey, Otis Redding
➤ Fave movie: *The Wizard of Oz* ("I have Dorothy stuff all over my room!")
➤ Fave subjects: English and history
➤ Hardest subjects: geometry and Spanish

So You Want to Know—

How Britney feels about her rise to fame? "I know I've had to give some stuff up to do this, but I don't miss high school. It's wonderful as long as you love what you're doing."

Britney Spears
Britney Fan Club
P.O. Box 250
Osyka, MS 39657

Shania Twain

*S*hania's road to success wasn't easy, to say the least. Born into a poor family in Canada, she worked hard to help her family in any way she could. Shania found time for her music, however, and while growing up she had the support of her parents, who shuttled her back and forth to auditions and jobs at all hours of the day or night. Her hard work has certainly paid off, and Shania is forever grateful to her family for her success.

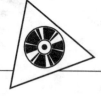

So You Want to Know—

Where the name Shania came from? Shania's stepfather was an Ojibwa Indian. In 1990, Shania was finally on her own after her siblings moved out and lightened her financial responsibilities. She shed her given name, Eileen, in favor of the Ojibwa name Shania, which means "I'm on my way."

Birthday Beat

August 28, 1965

Cool Credits

➤ Albums: *Shania Twain, The Woman in Me, Come On Over,* soundtracks for *Notting Hill, Aida*

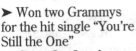

➤ Won two Grammys for the hit single "You're Still the One"

➤ *Come On Over* has been certified nine times platinum

➤ *Billboard*'s No. 1 Country Artist, 1996

➤ Accolades: American Music Awards for Favorite New Country Artist and Favorite Female Country Artist; Blockbuster Entertainment Awards; Canada's JUNO Awards; World Music Awards; Billboard Music Award, Female Artist of the Year; Hot 100 Singles Artist of the Year; Best-Selling Country Single of the Year ("You're Still the One"); one of *Entertainment Weekly*'s Entertainers of the Year, 1998

Super Stats

➤ Real name: Eileen Edwards

➤ Height: 5'4"

➤ Birthplace: Timmons, Ontario, Canada

➤ Family: husband is Robert John "Mutt" Lange, who is also her record producer; three younger siblings and one older sibling; parents, Clarence and Sharon Edwards; stepfather, Jerry Twain, adopted her when she was 4

Shania Twain
c/o Mercury Nashville
66 Music Square
West Nashville, TN 37203
Official Web site: www.shania-twain.com

Liv Tyler

▼▼▼▼▼▼▼▼▼▼▼▼▼▼▼▼▼▼▼

*T*all, slender, brunette, and exotic looking, Liv started out as a fashion model. Though she seemed to be on the fast track to success as a supermodel, Liv looked elsewhere for fulfillment. While filming a TV commercial in the Amazon jungle, she was bitten by a bug—the acting bug. Although her first few film experiences were discouraging, Liv stuck with it. She finally hit the big time when Bernardo Bertolucci, the Italian director, cast her in the lead of *Stealing Beauty* and her career took off.

Cool Credits

➤ Film: *Cookie's Fortune, Armageddon, Inventing the Abbotts, U-Turn, Stealing Beauty, That Thing You Do!, Empire Records, Heavy, Silent Fall*

➤ One of *People* magazine's 50 Most Beautiful People in the World, 1997

Super Stats

➤ Height: 5'10"
➤ Birthplace: Portland, Maine
➤ Family: daughter of Steven Tyler, lead singer of Aerosmith; half-sister, Mia Tyler, is a fashion model for Lane Bryant
➤ Name: Liv's mother named her after actress Liv Ullmann, who was on the cover of *TV Guide* the week Liv was born.
➤ Almost credit: Her cameo role in Woody Allen's musical comedy *Everyone Says I Love You* ended up on the cutting-room floor. She received a personal note from Woody, however, letting her know.

So You Want to Know—

Was Liv always an exotic beauty? Not really. Like many young people, Liv went through an awkward stage in her preteen years. Overweight, with a mouth full of braces, Liv didn't show all the signs of becoming a world-famous fashion model. By the time she hit 14, however, she was 5'10" and pretty enough to consider a career in modeling.

Birthday Beat
July 1, 1977

Liv Tyler
c/o J. Michael Bloom
233 Park Ave. South, 10th Floor
New York, NY 10003

James Van Der Beek

Identified as dyslexic in kindergarten, James has come a long way since. When a concussion stopped him from playing football at age 13, James landed a role as Danny in a school production of *Grease,* and the acting seed was planted. Not only is he now the hunky star of his own TV series, but he is also an honors student on an academic scholarship to college. Though he has put his pursuit of an English degree at Drew University in Madison, New Jersey, on hold to work on *Dawson's Creek,* James still spends a lot of his spare time reading and writing, and plans on returning to complete his studies someday.

So You Want to Know—

What kind of real-life training does James go through for his acting roles? He had to train with a dialogue coach to speak with a Texas accent for the film *Varsity Blues,* though thanks to his junior high football-playing days, he did most of his own throwing. "I can't let anybody do it all for me. It's one of those machismo things."

Birthday Beat
March 8, 1977

Super Stats

➤ Height: 6'
➤ Birthplace: Cheshire, Connecticut
➤ Nicknames: Baby James, Beek
➤ Name: *Van Der Beek* means "by the brook" in Dutch
➤ Family: oldest of three children; mother, Melinda, is a former Broadway dancer and runs a gymnastics studio; father, Jim, is a cellular phone salesman
➤ Hobbies: writing, playing guitar, sleeping, and playing all kinds of sports
➤ Fave book: *Portrait of the Artist as a Young Man* by James Joyce

Cool Credits

➤ One of *People* magazine's 50 Most Beautiful People in the World, 1998
➤ Film: *Varsity Blues; Harvest; I Love You, I Love You Not; Angus; Texas Rangers*
➤ TV: *Dawson's Creek;* appeared in *Clarissa Explains It All, The Red Booth*

James Van Der Beek
c/o *Dawson's Creek*
WB Network
4000 Warner Blvd.
Burbank, CA 91522

Ricky Williams

Known for his class and sportsmanship on the football field, Ricky commands respect from both his teammates and opponents. An honors student in high school and college, Ricky is a great role model for young kids. He spends his spare time visiting patients at the Austin Children's Hospital and serves as a mentor at a local elementary and middle school. "He's been such a classy guy," says Spike Dykes, coach for Texas Tech. "He's a good role model for a lot of people."

So You Want to Know—

If football is the most important thing in Ricky's life? Not completely. He places a high value on sportsmanship and education. Ricky passed up a chance at being the No. 5 draft pick for the NFL in order to finish his senior year of college.

Cool Credits

➤ Finished his college career with a total of 6,279 yards
➤ Won the Doak Walker Award
➤ Won the Heisman Trophy
➤ Career rushing yards in college: 4,573 (1995–97)
➤ Average yards per carry in college: 6.2
➤ Total touchdowns scored in college: 56

Super Stats

➤ Height: 6'
➤ Weight: 225
➤ Birthplace: San Diego, California
➤ College: University of Texas

Birthday Beat

May 21, 1977

➤ Family: twin sister, Cassie; another sister, Nisey; second cousin to Anaheim Angels designated hitter Cecil Fielder
➤ Drafted by the New Orleans Saints
➤ Fave saying: "Don't follow me. I may not lead. Don't lead me. I may not follow. Just walk next to me and be my friend."
➤ Fave musician: Bob Marley
➤ Inspiration: Doak Walker, 1948 Heisman trophy winner
➤ Language: speaks fluent Spanish
➤ Personal goals: to play both football and baseball professionally, and ultimately to become an elementary school teacher

Ricky Williams
c/o New Orleans Saints
5800 Airline Hwy.
Metairie, LA 70003

Venus and Serena Williams

▼▼▼▼▼▼▼▼▼▼▼▼▼▼▼▼▼▼▼

*V*enus and Serena Williams are on the fast track to becoming the most dominant sisters on the tennis court. They are already setting records in their young careers: They are the first sisters in professional tennis history to win singles titles in the same week. Their father, who is also their coach, stands proud as he watches both his daughters rise to sports stardom.

So You Want to Know—

Their nickname on the tennis circuit? The sisters are known as the Beaded Wonders. On the WTA tour, Serena was also called the Steamroller.

Birthday Beat

Venus: June 17, 1980
Serena: September 26, 1981

Cool Credits

➤ Won the French Open Women's Doubles tournament in 1999

➤ Became the first sisters in professional tennis history to win singles titles in the same week

➤ Serena was the singles semifinalist in Sydney in 1998

➤ Venus won the IGA Tennis Classic in 1998

➤ Serena won two mixed doubles tournaments with partner Max Mirnyi in 1998, her first professional year—Wimbledon and the U.S. Open

➤ Venus won Lipton Championships in 1998

Super Stats

➤ Heights: Venus—6'1"; Serena—5'10"

➤ Birthplaces: Venus—Lynwood, California; Serena—Saginaw, Michigan

➤ Current residence: Lynwood, California

➤ Family: father, Richard, is their coach

➤ Mixed doubles partners: Serena—Max Mirnyi; Venus—Justin Gimelstob

➤ Women's doubles partners: Venus and Serena are a successful doubles duo.

➤ Fun fact: An appointment at the hair salon for each sister can take up to four hours to change their braids and beads.

➤ Year turned pro: Venus—1995; Serena—1998

Venus and Serena Williams
c/o Corel WTA Tour
1266 E. Main St., 4th Floor
Stamford, CT 06902

Tiger Woods

Has he ever been seen *without* a golf club in his hand? At age 2, Tiger appeared on the *Mike Douglas Show* and putted with Bob Hope. He was featured in *Golf Digest* at 5 years of age, turned pro at age 20, and won the most prestigious tournament, the Masters, just two years later. Although he's already established himself as a living golf legend, he still has many more years to play, and may become the greatest golfer in history.

So You Want to Know—

Where Tiger got his name? He was named after Vuong Dang Phong, a Vietnamese soldier and friend of his father. Earl had given Vuong Dang the nickname Tiger, then passed it on to his only son.

Cool Credits

➤ Seven PGA Tour victories: 1998 BellSouth Classic, 1997 Mercedes Championship, the Masters, Byron Nelson Classic, Western Open, 1996 Walt Disney World Classic, Las Vegas Invitational

➤ Two international victories: 1998 Johnnie Walker Classic (Thailand), 1997 Asian Honda Classic (Thailand)

➤ PGA Player of the Year, 1997

➤ Won three U.S. Amateur Championships, 1994–96

➤ *Sports Illustrated*'s Sportsman of the Year, 1996

➤ PGA Rookie of the Year, 1996

➤ Led the PGA money list in 1997

Super Stats

➤ Real name: Eldrick Woods

➤ Height: 6'2"

➤ Birthplace: Cypress, California

➤ Current residence: Orlando, Florida

➤ Family: father, Earl, is a retired lieutenant colonel in the U.S. Army; mother, Kultida, is a native of Thailand

➤ Education: attended Stanford University

Birthday Beat
December 30, 1975

Tiger Woods
International Management Group
One Erieview Plaza, Suite 1300
Cleveland, OH 44114-1782
Official Web site: www.tigerwoods.com

Photo Credits

Cover:
Backstreet Boys/Gail A.P.R.F. © 1999 Shooting Star
Brandy/Ron Davis © 1999 Shooting Star
Terrell Davis/Brian Bahr © 1999 AllSport USA
Sarah Michelle Gellar/Terry Lilly © 1999 Shooting Star
Ricky Martin/Barry King © 1999 Shooting Star

Interior:
Pages 6, 14, 17, 26, 44, 82 & 86: Ron Davis © 1999 Shooting Star
Pages 8, 64 & 73: Paul Fenton © 1999 Shooting Star
Page 10: Gail/A.P.R.F. © 1999 Shooting Star
Pages 13, 19, 29, 35, 56, 76 & 89: Gary Marshall © 1999
    Shooting Star
Pages 20 & 46: Brian Bahr © 1999 AllSport USA
Page 22: Peter Taylor © 1999 AllSport USA
Page 25: Yoram Kahana © 1999 Shooting Star
Page 30: Tom Hauk © 1999 AllSport USA
Page 32: Otto Greule © 1999 AllSport USA
Pages 37, 48, 58 & 70: Mary Monaco © 1999 Shooting Star
Pages 38 & 92: Al Bello © 1999 AllSport USA
Page 41: Dorothy Low © 1999 Shooting Star
Page 42: Jed Jacobsohn © 1999 AllSport USA
Page 50: Rob Warner © 1999 Shooting Star
Page 52: Todd Warshaw © 1999 AllSport USA
Page 54: Barry King © 1999 Shooting Star
Page 60: Caserta/A.P.R.F. © 1999 Shooting Star
Page 62: Motown © 1999 Shooting Star
Page 66: Vincent Laforet © 1999 AllSport USA
Page 69: Tammy Calder © 1999 Shooting Star
Page 74: Howard Rosenberg © 1999 Shooting Star
Page 78: Vincent Frank © 1999 Shooting Star
Page 80: Harry How © 1999 AllSport USA
Page 85: P. Adress/A.P.R.F. © 1999 Shooting Star
Page 90: Stephen Dunn © 1999 AllSport USA
Page 92: Gary M. Prior © 1999 AllSport USA
Page 94: Jeff Shaw © 1999 Shooting Star